JOHN SCOTT

John A. Ives '00

Dalesman

Dalesman Publishing Company Ltd
Stable Courtyard, Broughton Hall,
Skipton, North Yorkshire BD23 3AZ
www.dalesman.co.uk

First Edition 2000

Text © John Scott
Illustrations © John Ives

Maps by Jeremy Ashcroft and Harry Salisbury

Cover: Minster and city walls by David Tarn

A British Library Cataloguing in Publication record
is available for this book

ISBN 1 85568 173 - 0

Printed by Amadeus Press, Huddersfield

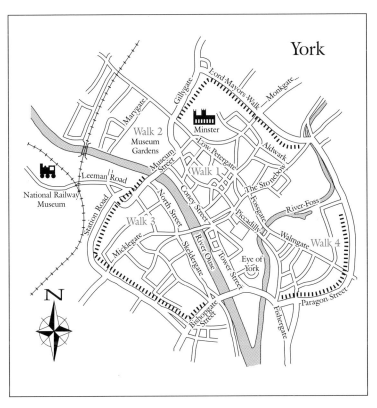

York

AUTHOR'S NOTE

The city has been divided into four walks. At the head of each one is a start/finish point and a brief résumé of what can be seen and the places that can be visited. Attractions are numbered in the text and on the accompanying maps for easy reference.

How long does each walk take? Impossible to say. The distances involved can be covered in less than an hour but the actual time taken depends on how long is spent stopping, shopping, staring and visiting. The Minster, the National Railway Museum and the Castle Museum, for instance, can each take hours to explore in detail. The longest walk – right round the city on the bar walls – lasts about 90 minutes.

Introduction

A walk through York is a walk through the history of England. But unlike other tourist cities which lock their history away in museums the best things in York are free – the Minster, the medieval walls and the narrow streets. They stir images of invading Romans, pillaging Vikings, bustling medieval markets, the clash of Roundheads and Cavaliers and of elegant Georgian ladies dancing the night away after a day at the races.

The unique attraction of the city can be found in the way that every age has left behind a little piece of itself for later generations to admire. The Romans have a tower and a section of wall still standing in the Museum Gardens; the remains of Viking houses are in Coppergate; there are medieval churches and ancient halls and merchants' homes, Georgian residences and a proud 'temple to steam' in memory of the men who built the railways. But the ingredients that make up this unique city are not just those of history, architecture, art and culture. York in recent years has quietly turned itself into a superb shopping centre thanks, it has to be admitted, to the tourist trade. As a result a cultural browse through the history of England, by wandering the streets of York, can easily be combined with some very sophisticated shopping. In fact it has something for everyone as well as being the perfect city to be explored on foot …

Jon A. Ives '00

History

It was a Roman general pushing northwards to subdue the troublesome Brigantes who founded York in AD 71. Quintus Petilius Cerialis recognised a good defensive position when he saw one. He ordered the men of the Ninth Legion to dig ditches and erect the ramparts of a wood-walled fortress in a fork of land between two rivers – the Ouse and the Foss. Wooden pallisades soon gave way to imposing stone walls and towers and the soldiers stayed on – for four centuries. A distant outpost of the Roman Empire became the northern capital of Britain. And when campaigning Emperors took up residence it was from here that the whole 'civilised' world was governed.

A glimpse of the grandeur that was Roman York can be seen in the Multangular Tower in the Museum Gardens. The rest of the fortress lies buried beneath the modern city – the legionary headquarters lying under the Minster. It can still be seen by paying a visit to the cathedral 'basement'. A collapsed pillar from the colonnaded HQ was retrieved during foundation repairs and now stands, re-erected, outside the Minster's south door. Nearby sits a brooding statue of Constantine the Great who was proclaimed Emperor here. (Walk One).

Anglo Saxons moved into the remains of the Roman city in the fifth century and Eboracum became Eoferwic. The first cathedral – made of wood – was built in 627 only to be destroyed six years later by warring factions. St Cuthbert built another this time in stone. A relic of this turbulent period can be found behind the City Library (Walk Two) in the shape of an Anglian tower which was part of the Anglo Saxon city defences. It had been covered over for centuries by later earthworks thrown up to defend the city. Amidst all these upheavals Alcuin the Scholar became Master of the School of St Peter at York before moving on to even greater fame at Charlemagne's Court at Aachen.

After the Anglo Saxons the Vikings swept in – plundering, pillaging and eventually settling. York became a Viking city – Eric Bloodaxe being one of its more colourful rulers. Under yet another name – Jorvik – the city became a lusty, bustling, commercial centre. The lifestyle of Jorvik's inhabitants came vividly to life when an excavation in Coppergate revealed streets of Viking homes, artefacts and even debris from their dinner tables. This world can still be seen – reconstructed on the site where it was found – in the famous Jorvik Viking Centre.

York also had a part to play during the events of the most famous date in English history – 1066. King Harold galloped into York with his house carls to confront an invading Nordic army led by his half brother, Tostig. He had no sooner defeated him at Stamford Bridge when the news came that William the Bastard, soon to be William the Conqueror, had landed at Hastings. What might have happened at Hastings if Harold had not been so exhausted by his enforced trip to Yorkshire is one of the great 'ifs' of English history.

William subdued the south but the north was made of sterner stuff. He began a ruthless "harrying of the North". Clifford's Tower on its huge mound and its smaller twin at Baile Hill survive as a relic of the brutal efficiency of the Norman invader's methods for quelling resistance.

Medieval times saw the city taking on its present street form and becoming a centre of power and trade. At its heart the present cathedral was being built – 250 years in the making and completed in July 1472. Much of the stone arrived by river and was taken to the site along the Roman Via Praetoria soon to become known as Stonegate (Walk One). During the Wars of the Roses the head of the Duke of York decorated a spike on Micklegate Bar.(Walk Two). "So that York may overlook the town of York," to quote Shakespeare's Henry VI.

But York also saw the reconciliation that followed the conflict with the marriage in the Minster in 1486 of Henry VII and Elizabeth of York, an event commemorated in the red and white roses in the design of the Rose Window in the South Transept. In the more peaceful periods between wars and plagues rich merchants formed powerful craft guilds and built themselves grand halls from which to conduct their business – Merchant Adventurers', Merchant Taylors' (See Walk One and Two). And they surrounded their bustling city with the defensive walls that still stand today. Art and culture flourished – architecture, stained glass and the city's famous Medieval Mystery Plays, the story of the world from the Creation to the Last Trump performed on pageant wagons in the streets. They have been periodically revived in recent years with great success in York Festivals.

During the Civil War Charles I had a printing press in St William's College (Walk Two). It turned out leaflets or 'paper bullets' as part of his propaganda campaign. When the Parliamentarians besieged the city in 1645 they turned their cannon on the city walls. The Royalist cause was in desperate straits but Prince Rupert galloped to the rescue. The cheering did not last long, however, for the garrison and Rupert marched out and confronted the Roundheads in battle at Marston Moor a few miles away – and lost. The Royalist survivors streamed back to York only to have the gates of Micklegate Bar (Walk Two) shut in their faces. In hot pursuit was the Parliamentarian leader, Sir Thomas Fairfax. The Roundheads had a passion for smashing 'idolatrous' stained glass windows but fortunately for York Sir Tom was a Yorkshireman. He kept his men firmly in hand and the Minster's glass survived.

In Georgian times the races, the trials at the assize courts and the popular public hangings that often followed, made York the centre of the North's social life. Fine town houses were erected such as Fairfax House (Walk One) as well as public buildings like the Debtors' Prison and the Mansion House (Walk One). The Assembly Rooms (Walk One) was built by public subscription so the aristocracy could meet, dance and socialise in elegant splendour. The theatre thrived. And for the common folk there was the entertainment of seeing prisoners paraded through the city to the gallows on Knavesmire. A new 'drop' near St George's Field, now a car park, was just as popular and gave the prisoners a shorter walk to eternity. The ballad sellers nevertheless did a brisk trade en route. Dick Turpin's cell can be seen in the Castle Museum (Walk One) next door to the court where he was tried.

Victorian times brought the mixed blessing of the age of steam to the city. Iron Corinthian pillars and graceful arches decorated the ornate 'new' railway station – now a listed building (Walk Two).

The first temporary station halted the track just outside the city walls. The second saw a gap torn through the ramparts and a new station built inside. But this soon proved too cramped for the growing popularity of 'going by train'. Greater public mobility and the novelty of having breakfast in York and tea in the capital saw the north's aristocratic social scene drift away to London. The railways, however, did bring trade and the Victorian age saw the creation of one of the city's major industries, confectionery, with the establishment of the Rowntree's and Terry's factories.

And in more modern times …

Railways and chocolates provided the backbone to York's 20th century economy until 1951 when almost by chance and good luck a third was added – tourism. The city was chosen as a regional celebration centre for the Festival of Britain. The medieval Mystery Plays were revived after a lapse of 400 years to great critical acclaim. And the city kept getting itself into the news – in 1961 the Duke of Kent married Miss Katherine Worsley in a white rose wedding in the cathedral – a huge, televised Royal occasion. In 1968 the Minster's central tower was found to be in danger of collapse causing national concern. And the city's 1900th birthday party in 1971 had the Queen as its guest of honour and the Household Cavalry riding through the streets. When Viking York was discovered in an excavation in Coppergate in 1976 and most of the crowned heads of Scandinavia came to visit there was no stopping the burgeoning tourist trade.

And as if the city had not received enough media exposure an act of God in 1984 put it back into the news yet again. It came in the shape of a shaft of lightning that set the south transept of the Minster ablaze. The pictures of the fire and its aftermath were seen around the world with the result that the rebuilt transept comes high on every visitor's 'must see' list.

After a cool start the locals have learned to accept the drawbacks of tourism – a high season of crowded streets, full car parks and busy shops – and to enjoy instead the benefits: more jobs and better amenities. The economic success of the city has attracted Government departments northwards and this has diversified the economy still further. York now has a cosmopolitan air about it as well as an acute awareness of the debt it owes to its history.

The Minster and heart of the city

Start/Finish: York Minster, visiting the Shambles,
guild halls, museums and shops

The Shambles

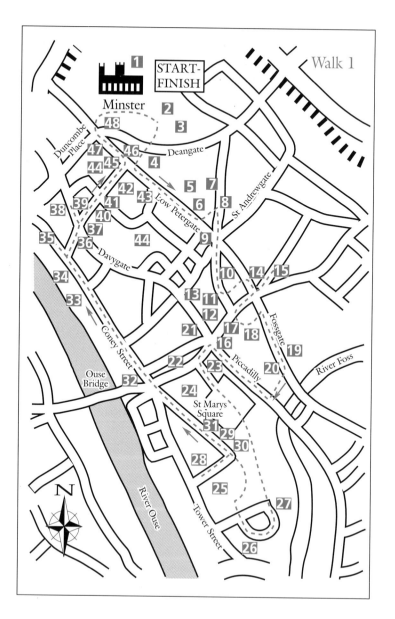

START-
FINISH

Walk 1

1

Minster

2

3

48

Duncombe Place

Deangate

47 46
44 45
4
42
43
39
38 41
40
37
44
35 36
Davygate

5 7
6 8

St. Andrewgate
Low Petergate

9

10 14 15

13 11
12

17 18
16

21

22

23 Piccadilly

19

20

Fossgate

River Foss

Ouse
Bridge

32

24

St Marys
Square

31 29
30

28

25

27

26

River Ouse

Tower Street

N

12

Enter the **Minster** (1) by the door in the north west tower. Visitors are immediately struck by the sheer size of the building and by a feeling of airy lightness to set against the powerful, colourful imagery of the huge stained glass windows. This is the largest Gothic cathedral north of the Alps, a treasure house of history and architecture spanning nearly 2,000 years and which attracts some 2,250,000 visitors a year. There is so much to see it is best to collect one of the many leaflets available and select one's own particular interest. From the roof – after climbing 279 twisting steps – there is a magnificent view over the pantiled city. In the 'basement' can be seen the ruins of a Roman legionary fortress and two earlier Norman churches as well as the modern steel-reinforced concrete feet which support the central tower.

For a more detailed description of the cathedral and what to look out for see page 41.

Leave the cathedral by the South Transept door. Immediately to the left is a seated statue of **Constantine the Great** (2) who was proclaimed Emperor of the Roman World at York in 306AD. Diagonally across the road to the left is a re-erected **stone column** (3) from the Roman headquarters. The drums of stone were found collapsed under the cathedral when excavation work was carried out to save the central tower from collapse in 1968. Cross the road and enter **Minster Gates** (4) so called because it was the site of one of the four gates through a 12ft high wall which circled the cathedral precincts.

Look back and upwards at the Rose Window in the gable end of the South Transept. This was the window which narrowly escaped destruction in the fire of 1984. It became the inspiring symbol for the rebuilding of the transept.

Turn left along **Low Petergate** (5) once the Via Principia of Eboracum, and now an attractive street of Tudor and Stuart houses with overhanging upper storeys and shops below. The medieval pageant wagons followed this route and had one of their 'stations' here to entertain the families of rich merchants watching from their upper windows. Look out for and take a turning into a narrow entrance on the left. This is **Horn Pot Lane** (6) named after a local industry based on items made of horn and is one of York's many narrow, twisting snickleways.

Opposite Horn Pot Lane is another snickleway – Mad Alice Lane named after Alice Smith whose reputed madness did not prevent her from being hung in the 1830s.

Turn down Horn Pot Lane which leads into the church yard of **Holy Trinity**, Goodramgate (7) – the most atmospheric small church in the city with its uneven, tombstone-laden floor and its venerable box pews. A valet who attended Charles I lies buried beneath an inscribed stone in front of the communion rails.

(Gates into Horn Pot Lane are locked on Sundays, Mondays and in the evenings – in which case continue straight along Petergate into King's Square.)

Leave the church yard by the wrought iron gates into Goodramgate and on the left is **Lady's Row** (8) a line of 14th century houses – the oldest surviving row of houses in York. Directly opposite can be seen what might have happened to York if local conservationists had not stepped in.

It was here that a row of old houses was pulled down and replaced with modern brick and concrete shop fronts. There was such an outcry that tight controls were put on all future city centre development.

Turn right when in Goodramgate and after a few yards turn left into **King's Square** (9) – the outdoor entertainment and alfresco eating centre of the city – fish and chips being the top item on the menu. During the summer the buskers keep the crowds amused while nearby food outlets provide the nourishment for tourists and eventually the pigeons.

(Other cafes, particularly in St Sampson's Square, have been following suit recently and spilling out onto the pavement – French style.)

King's Square only came into being in 1937 with the demolition of the redundant Holy Trinity Church. Today jugglers, fire-eaters and monocyclists entertain over the gravestones. The square's name probably comes from a Viking king's court which is thought to have been in the area.

In the south east corner of the square is the entrance to the **Shambles** (10) and a glimpse of what York must have been like in late medieval times. The timber houses lean affectionately towards one another across the narrow street – so close in places that one can shake hands with your neighbour across the road by leaning out of the bedroom window. This used to be the street of the butchers, the name being a corruption of fleshammels – the ledges for displaying meat. Now these are the window sills of shops all of them devoted to the tourist trade. The ledges are very fragile. Don't sit on them !

In the Shambles at **No 35** (11) is the home and shrine of a butcher's wife, who was pressed to death in 1586 for harbouring priests. She was canonised in 1970 as St Margaret Clitheroe of York. At No 40 is **Butchers' Hall** (12).

Narrow alleys on the right provide access to the **Newgate Market** (13) where traders still set out their stalls as their ancestors have done for centuries. In medieval times York market was so popular that houses were demolished to make room for more stalls.

Take the narrow archway on the left, however, and this leads into the city's shortest street (35 yards) but the one with the longest name – **Whipmawhopmagate** (14). Opinions differ about where the name comes from. Some say it was medieval local dialect for 'What a street!' Others say it was because public whippings took place in nearby Pavement.

A short detour here if you like 'hands on' archaeology. Go straight ahead down St Saviourgate to the former church of St Saviour which has become the ARC, the **Archaeological Resource Centre** (15) (See page 41). Here young and old would-be archaeologists can try their hand at sorting out 'dig debris' and learning medieval crafts like shoe-making.

Return to the street with the long name and turn left and right into **Pavement** (16) – logically so called because it was the first street in the city to be paved. This is where the extended medieval markets used to be held and they would have made handy but noisy neighbours for the well-to-do occupants of **Herbert House** (17) – the finest example of black and white half timbering in the city. The Lord Mayor of London, Christopher Herbert, bought the site and the house was built about 1620. Sir Thomas Herbert, valet to Charles I, who accompanied the king to his execution, was born here. As with many of the fine old buildings in the city the ground floor is occupied by shops.

Alongside the house is yet another snickleway and yet another glimpse of what York looked like centuries ago. **Lady Peckitt's Yard** (18) is a cluster of Tudor black and white houses, some of them making a bridge over the lane.

The name of the alleyway comes somewhat snidely from a Lady Mayoress of the city in 1702. A local saying went that while "the mayor is a lord for a year and a day his wife is a lady for ever and aye." So Lady Peckitt is remembered while her husband, the Lord Mayor John Peckitt, is virtually forgotten. Emerging from the Yard into Fossgate, turn right, and pass the former **Electric Cinema** (19) (now a furniture store) which presents a Venetian-style half-domed face to the world in terracotta tiles – a startling piece of early 20th century architecture in an old street.

Further down Fossgate on the right look out for an imposing stone gateway topped by a coat of arms bearing two winged horses and the motto: Dieu Nous Donne Bonne Aventure. Freely translated: God give us some good business opportunities. This is the entrance to the **Merchant Adventurers' Hall** (20) a magnificent timber-framed building from which the powerful Adventurers' Guild controlled much of the trade of the city in medieval times. Guild meetings are still held here and the occasional candlelit dinner.

Leave the hall and walk round to the front of the building and up the steps into Piccadilly. Turn right and head the few yards towards a busy crossroads. Straight ahead is what locals irreverently call the Splash Palace – a somewhat grand building block containing toilets

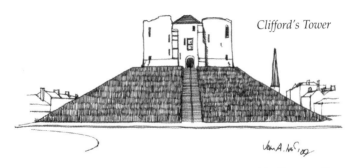

Clifford's Tower

and offices. Behind it lies the tree lined expanse of **Parliament Street** (21) with its seats and fountain making it a creditable imitation of a French *place* surrounded by stores and banks. On a fine day it is a pleasant and bustling place to sit, eat, and often be entertained by yet more buskers.

But instead turn left into Coppergate. On your right is **All Saints, Pavement** (22) which is mentioned in the Domesday Book and has a lantern top tower from which a light still shines every night. Its original purpose was to act as a lighthouse to guide travellers towards the city through the dark perils of the Forest of Galtres. Nearly forty Lord Mayors of York are buried in the church. The Merchant Adventurers process to All Saints once a year to listen to a sermon reminding them to 'think of their latter end'. Another reminder of death is on the church's door knocker which is in the form of a sinner being eaten by a lion.

After visiting All Saints return to Coppergate and cross into a new street, **Coppergate Walk** (23). This land was once occupied by a sweet factory. When the site was cleared for rebuilding, the archaeologists moved in and struck gold – the remains of a Viking city with the wooden walls of some buildings still standing nearly two metres high. The site is now covered with shops but underground, where the finds were made, the city of Jorvik has been recreated in the **Jorvik Viking Centre** (24). Time cars take visitors through the sights and smells of the past. (See page 42)

Pass the modern shops and go across the small square which is surrounded by modern stores and take a pavement exit in the far right corner. This takes you within sight of some of William the Conqueror's grimmer handiwork, **Clifford's Tower** (25). After his victory at Hastings, William began what the chroniclers graphically called the "harrying of the North". This huge mound of earth topped then by a wooden castle was part of the process. Northerners, helped by the Danes, burned it down. William rebuilt it and the north too eventually had to submit.

The castle was in flames again in 1190 when the city's Jewish community took refuge there during anti-Semitic riots. Some 150 died and there is now a plaque to their memory at the foot of the mound. In the 17th century the tower was used for storing gunpowder. An explosion blew off the roof leaving it as it is today – not much to see inside but fine views from the top.

Walk through the car park past the tower and into a three-sided courtyard of Georgian buildings. **The Law Courts** (26) are on the right and the **Castle Museum** (27) on the left and straight ahead. The building facing you, which is part of the Museum, is the former Debtors' Prison: "no place for man to thrive," says an inscription on the wall. This was grimly true for people were thrown in here for debt and kept there until they, or more likely their relatives, paid up. The building on the left is the former Female Prison. Both prisons were converted into a museum in 1938 to display something of Yorkshire's social history based on a collection of everyday things gathered together by Dr John Kirk on his travels in and around Pickering. The former female exercise yard has been transformed into a Victorian cobbled street. The cramped cells of the debtors' prison now house craft workshops. In 1735 one of these cells housed Dick Turpin who was sentenced to death in the law courts next door and hung on St George's Fields nearby. (More details on the museum – See page 42.)

Retrace your steps across the car park and beyond the tower turn left into Tower Street. Here is the **Regimental Museum** (28) of two famous regiments – 4th/7th Dragoon Guards and the Prince of Wales's Own Regiment of Yorkshire. (See page 42)

On leaving the museum turn left and left again into Castlegate. Immediately on the right one can now discover what it was like to live in Georgian elegance. **Fairfax House** (29) was rescued by the York Civic Trust and with furniture donated by Noel Terry, the great grandson of the founder of Terry's of York, it was restored and refurnished and set back in time to the days of its original owner in the 1750s – Viscount Fairfax. The result is one of the finest furnished Georgian houses in England. (See page 42)

And next door is the entrance to the former **St George's Cinema** (30). The cinema has long gone but the Greek style entrance created in 1911 has been preserved as a 'modern' addition to the intriguing multi mix of architecture that makes up the city.

Continue up Castlegate and on the right is **St Mary's,** Castlegate (31) which has the tallest spire in the city.

At the end of Castlegate go straight ahead over the busy traffic junction and into Spurriergate and then Coney Street. This is the main shopping centre of the city although other areas such as Coppergate Walk are now in strong competition. **Coney Street** (32) is a corruption of the Danish for King's Street and although difficult to imagine today it was once the stopping place for stage coaches. To travel from here to London took four days.

Further along the street, past the large stores, one sees the perky figure of a 17th century admiral in full regalia 'shooting the sun' with a sextant. He stands above the huge clock of **St Martin-le-Grand** (33) which is suspended above the road on cast-iron brackets. St Martin's itself was destroyed by the Luftwaffe during the Second World War and the admiral had his coat tails singed in the fire. He was repaired and the church partially restored as a memorial to local people who died in the war.

Coney Street gives way to St Helen's Square, a pleasant sitting out area overlooked by the Mansion House and fashionable tea rooms.

York proudly boasts that its Lord Mayor had a **Mansion House** (34) in 1730, ten years before the Lord Mayor of London had his. With its attractive Georgian facade and window boxes it is still the home for the Lord Mayor of York during his term of office and can still be visited. (See page 42)

Take the passage alongside the Mansion House (note the hooks in the ceiling for hanging game to keep it cool) and walk down to the **Guildhall** (35) and its adjoining council offices. There have been council buildings on this spot since the 13th century although the present Common Hall is a replica. The original was destroyed in the same bombing raid which burned down St Martin-le-Grand.

In one of the surviving chambers, however, Committee Room No 1, the Roundheads met the Scots and paid cash for the handing over of Charles I who had taken refuge in Scotland after the Civil War. The silver was carefully counted out on the table.

Back in St Helen's Square and you are standing at the grand entrance to Roman York. Traces of its walls and towers were found in excavations under the street. One of the tea rooms in the square,

Mansion House

Betty's (36), has its own place in more recent history. During the Second World War it was a meeting place for off-duty RAF air crew from the nearby bomber airfields. Many of them scratched their names on the bar room mirror where they can still be seen today.

In the corner of the square is **St Helen's Church** (37) where the coat of arms of the glass painters' guild can be seen in the west window of the south aisle. It is there because many of the glass painters who worked on the Minster windows lived in this area.

And now a short detour to the left up Blake street to the **Assembly Rooms** (38) the social centre of the city in Georgian times. With its double row of marbled columns the inside of the building looks like an ornate Egyptian temple. The columns were not to the taste of one 17th century aristocrat who complained that they were too narrow for her wide hooped skirts. Return to St Helen's Square and turn left into **Stonegate** (39) arguably the finest street in York – a place where history and shopping are close companions and jostle each other for attention. Grooves cut by Roman chariots were found in the paving beneath the present street and this was the route along which stone was dragged from the river to the cathedral.

(There can be confusion with York street names because of their Scandinavian roots. 'Gate' does not mean gate but street and 'bar' means gate.)

Outside No 32 is a plaque claiming that Guy Fawkes was born 'hereabouts'. On the right is the **Old Punch Bowl Inn** (40), one of the oldest inns in the city, and where the Gimcrack Club, a gathering of racing gentlemen, first held their annual meetings. The Gimcrack Stakes are still run on Knavesmire. On the left is a narrow, snickleway entrance to an almost hidden covered shopping street – the Stonegate Arcade. It is almost hidden because town planners, not surprisingly, refused to knock down old property in Stonegate to give it a wider entrance.

A topless angel graces the corner of a half timbered shop front at the entrance to Little Stonegate on the opposite side of the street. She was not always so shamelessly on display but graced the prow of a sailing ship. She looks down on **Mulberry Hall** (41) the 15th century town house of a former bishop which now serves teas to visitors upstairs while selling fine porcelain below.

On the right yet another snickleway – **Coffee Yard** (42) with a red carved 'printer's devil' on the entrance post. The real 'devils' were the boys who carried the type for the city's first newspaper which was printed hereabouts. Laurence Sterne, the writer, was a customer in the coffee shops that thrived in this area.

In Coffee Yard the home of a 15th century York goldsmith, Alderman William Snawsell, has been restored as **Barley Hall** (43) (See page 42)

Return to Stonegate and head towards yet another venerable drinking haunt the **Olde Starre Inn** (44) which has its sign hung right across the street. A narrow passage on the left leads to the inn where Royalists probably caroused during the Siege of York for it is mentioned in the pamphlets they printed at that time. Almost as one leaves Stonegate a doorway numbered 52A on the left leads into a passage and to the remains of the **Norman House** (45) built in 1180. It is the oldest house in the city but sadly has just two walls standing set into the stonework of other buildings.

You are back at Minster Gates with the Rose Window of the South Transept again looking down at you and a carving of **Minerva** (46) leaning on a pile of books watching you from above a shop window. As the goddess of wisdom she symbolises the bookshops which once filled this area. Turn left into Low Petergate and on the left is another old house, now a hotel, (47), the reputed birthplace of **Guy Fawkes.** On the right is most certainly the place where he was christened for his name, Guy, son of Edward Fawkes, is in the register of **St Michael-le-Belfrey** (48) and dated April 16, 1570. Step outside St Michael's and you are back at the Minster. One has to thank Charles I for this fine open view of the West Front. On one of his visits he found it obscured and cluttered by cottages some of which were built against the walls of the cathedral. He ordered the cottages to be pulled down. The Minster authorities complied but waited until all the leases, and consequently all the rents, had ceased.

A view from the walls and a walk in the park

Start/Finish: Minster to Museum Gardens/National Railway Museum. En route: St William's College, Treasurer's House, Merchant Taylors' Hall, onto the bar walls, King's Manor, Art Gallery, Museum Gardens and National Railway Museum.

Bootham Bar

Jan A. Ives '00

From the steps of the Minster's south transept turn left and follow the path around the east end of the cathedral – a route known as the **Queen's Path** (49) ever since Queen Elizabeth II visited the city in 1972 to distribute the Royal Maundy money. Facing you is the medieval black and white timbered facade of **St William's College** (50) named after a relative of William the Conqueror who was Archbishop of York in 1153. It was the home of priests serving the Minster until they were dispossessed by order of Henry VIII and the

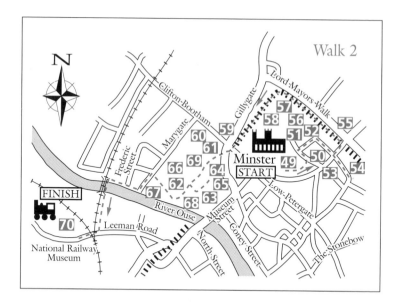

building passed into private hands. It stands in College Street, formerly known as Vicars' Lane. One owner was Charles I who set up a printing press here in an attempt to win the propaganda campaign of the Civil War by printing leaflets. It is now the cathedral's Visitors' Centre.

After leaving St William's College turn right and right again into the cobbled Chapter House Street which runs alongside the walled garden of **Treasurer's House** (51). The house was built in 1491 as a home for the Minster's treasurers but saw many owners before the Yorkshire industrialist, Frank Green, took possession and restored the building at the beginning of this century. It was taken over by the National Trust in 1930 and apart from its fine furniture has collections of china, pottery and glass. It can also boast not one but a cohort of ghosts who were seen marching across the cellars by a workman doing repairs. Ghoulishly they were only visible from the knees up – their hobnailed boots apparently marching along on the Roman road which is known to lie under the building.

Turn left from the exit of the house and continue along the cobbled street and turn right into Ogleforth.

Standing isolated because of the demolition of other properties is the strange, brick-built 17th century structure called the **Dutch House** (52). The Great Fire of London and memories of the siege of York apparently provoked a demand for homes less likely to go up in flames. As local builders lacked expertise in working with brick they are thought to have met the demand by borrowing Dutch building techniques and style.

Cross the road immediately ahead (Goodramgate) and go into **Aldwark** (53) a name meaning old fortifications. More remains of the old Roman wall have been found here. To the right smart, modern town houses have replaced what was a few decades ago a semi-derelict area of warehouses and empty property. To the left, set in its own grounds, is yet another of the city's old guild halls – **Merchant Taylors'** (54). York's tailors, drapers and hosiers amalgamated in 1662 to form the Merchant Taylors' Guild and they took over this Great Hall which had been built in the 14th century. (See page 43)

Retrace your footsteps to Goodramgate and turn right to **Monk Bar**

St William's College

(55). Take the narrow staircase inside the wall on the left hand side and at the top turn left and go onto the parapet walk.

To the right is a small museum which might help you decide if Richard III was a good king or the monster portrayed by Shakespeare. (See page 43)

This ancient gateway dates from the 14th century and some of its rooms were used as a prison. The stone figures on the roof who are frozen in the act of throwing stones were supposed to make night attackers think they were sentries.

Here begins a semi-aerial view of pantiled rooftops and gardens with the Minster as their backdrop.

The first gardens one sees are of **Grays Court** (56) (an extension of Treasurer's House) where the besieged Royalists had their war room. On the opposite side, looking over the battlements, the grassy bank that supports the wall is covered with daffodils in springtime. Not so in medieval days. This was where the town 'privies' were dumped and butchers' offal was thrown out of the city. The smell became so obnoxious that the City Fathers had the practice banned. The parapet walk now takes a sharp turn to the left. Looking within the city the fine brick building with its well cared for gardens is the **Deanery** (57). During the 12th and 13th century an archbishop's palace occupied much of the open land behind the cathedral at this point. The stone built chapel, now the **Minster Library** (58) is the only substantial structure remaining from this period. It stands in Dean's Park the expansive lawned area behind the cathedral. Continue along the parapet. The houses and backyards of Gillygate are crushed against the outside of the ramparts but there are more fine views of the Minster inside the walls. You eventually reach **Bootham Bar** (59) where traitors' heads were 'spiked' to encourage loyalty among the King's subjects. In those days the Forest of Galtres came almost up to the walls and armed guides waited here in the bar to take travellers through the forest. They had to be armed to ward off the wolves. The Romans of course were here first and the gateway stands on their gateway, the Prima Porta Dextra.

(In the early 1800s a gap was torn in York's medieval defensive wall here to make way for a new entrance into the city – St Leonard's. The 'walkable wall' resumes across the river alongside Lendal Bridge. See Walk Three.)

Descending from Bootham Bar you are in Exhibition Square with its fountain and statue of York artist, William Etty, famous and infamous for his paintings of nudes. Some of his works are in the nearby **Art Gallery** (60) (See page 43) along with paintings covering some six hundred years of European art. Etty was among those who successfully campaigned against proposals to pull down Bootham Bar.

On the left is **King's Manor** (61) the former home of the Abbot of St Mary's until it was taken over by the Crown when Henry VIII closed down the monasteries. The king made it the headquarters for the Council of the North. Since then it has had a succession of Royal residents including not just Henry but James I, Charles I and Charles II. Charles I's ornate coat of arms is carved in stone above the entrance. Today the University of York is in residence.

Take a lane to the left of Kings Manor and there is a forlorn and isolated section of the town wall on your left. Before entering the **Museum Gardens** (62) take a path up the earth ramparts on the left and go through a small gap in the wall. It is here that the layers of history that make up the York story can clearly be seen. To the right is the **Multangular Tower** (63) the south west corner bastion of Roman York. The Roman stonework, however, only goes up to a height of six metres – the rest of the masonry is medieval. Along the wall to the left layers of the present embankment have been cut away to show the different levels of previous defensive walls. Deep within the embankment was found an **Anglian Tower** (64) thought to have been built in the seventh or eighth century and which lay undiscovered until excavations this century. Scholars, however, are now questioning whether the tower is Anglian – it might be even older and from the late Roman period.

In front of you as you come through the wall are the few remains of the medieval **St Leonard's Hospital** (65). The hospital, which once covered a huge expanse of land, was the subject of a 'dig' by the television Time Team.

King's Manor

Return through the hole in the wall and turn left into the **Museum Gardens**. This pleasant expanse of lawns and trees (66) (an ideal place for a summer picnic) was once covered with the buildings of one of the largest and wealthiest Benedictine centres in the country – St Mary's Abbey. All that remains of the abbey church is the ruined north aisle. It has been used as a stage setting for the city's medieval Mystery Plays with 'angels' appearing in the window arches and devils romping across the grass-covered nave. Over the centuries most of the abbey buildings disappeared as people stole or bought the masonry for building work. The exception is the **Hospitium** (67) – the abbot's guest house – which has been restored and is used for exhibitions. Hidden among the trees is a tiny astronomical **observatory** (68) with a revolving roof which was designed by John Smeaton who built the Eddystone Lighthouse. The Yorkshire Philosophical Society commissioned its construction following the inaugural meeting of the British Association for the Advancement of Science in 1831. Its use, however, is now severely restricted because of light spill from the city streets.

Set on a stone podium overlooking the gardens is the imposing Greek facade of the **Yorkshire Museum** (69). Archaeological, geological and natural history items are stored here (including the Middleham jewel) and in the basement is a display which recaptures the life of the monks who lived here. (See page 43)

The walk can end at this point or can be continued to take in the **National Railway Museum** (70). To reach the Museum leave the Gardens by the path to the south of the abbey ruins and walk into Marygate. Turn left and go down towards the river.

On your left is part of the massive stone wall with which the monks surrounded their 12 acre home. The abbey was outside the main city defences but within the York boundaries – a situation which caused numerous disputes between the abbot and the city authorities.

Close to the river bank are the city's more modern defences – against flooding. They include a wall recessed into the road which can be raised to keep out the River Ouse. Turn right and walk along the river bank and take the footbridge alongside the railway bridge over the River Ouse. On the far bank turn left and then right into the narrow lane that leads at right angles away from the river. On reaching the main road turn right again underneath the main London – Scotland railway line and you are at the National Railway Museum. (See page 43)

Railways, Roundheads and churches

Start/finish: Lendal Bridge. The Bar Walls, Micklegate, Ouse Bridge and All Saints, North Street. (Includes the first stage of a complete walk around the Bar walls —See Walk 4.)

*The Stocks,
Holy Trinity*

Lendal Bridge (71) is modern in York terms. For centuries people crossed the river at this point but by ferry. The bridge had to be built in 1862 to meet the demand for a better access to the 'new' railway station. On the northern bank is **Lendal Tower** (72) from which a London entrepreneur in 1677 supplied the city with piped water, the pipes being hollowed-out tree trunks. For three days half the city had water and then the supply was switched to the other half for another three days. Some of the old pumping machinery and wooden pipes are still in the tower. Chains were hung across the river from this tower to **Barker Tower** (73) on the south bank so that traders could not evade ship tolls. Bodies recovered from the river were housed in Barkers Tower but in recent years it has had more pleasant uses either for storage or as a craft shop.

Leave the pavement and go up onto the parapet walk of the Bar Walls. The Romans built their fortress on the northern side of the river but a town soon developed on the southern bank. This section of the medieval walls follows the line of the defences that were put around this Roman civilian settlement. And here begins another semi-aerial view of the city – this time taking in the history of the railways. The wall crosses over two busy roads and on the left is the headquarters of the former North Eastern Railway built in 1906. The white obelisk is part of the **War Memorial** (74) dedicated to railwaymen killed in World War One. Looking down over the battlements away from the city one sees an area of grass, trees and gravestones incongruously laid out alongside a busy road. This is the **Cholera Graveyard** (75) where victims of an epidemic in 1832 are buried. Developers avoided the site for fear of reawakening the disease so the graveyard remained untouched and has become an historical curiosity. Beyond the road and in the gardens of the **Royal York Hotel**, Roman graves (76) were found in recent excavations – confirming the Roman custom of burying their dead outside town. Look back now at the famous picture postcard view of York – the ramparts sloping away in front of you and with the cathedral in the distance.

Looking over the battlements one sees York's own 'temple of steam', the **Railway Station** (77), considered one of the finest examples of Victorian railway architecture in the country with its graceful curved roof and Corinthian pillars. This is the third York railway station. The first was a temporary affair just outside the walls which was quickly outgrown. A hole was therefore cut through the medieval ramparts and the railway line ran underneath the wall to a 'new' railway station – where offices now stand. This site too became so cramped that the present railway station had to be built in 1877. Not all the Victorian shareholders were happy about the scheme. One called it a 'splendid monument of extravagance".

Close to the 'big' railway station are several small ones in the **Model Railway Exhibition** (78) (See page 43)

Continue along the rampart walk to the Royal entrance to York – **Micklegate Bar** (79). This gateway has seen some of the most dramatic moments in the city's history. Built between the 12th and 14th centuries it stands across the ancient route from London into York.

A succession of monarchs have passed this way but all royal 'visits' have not been happy ones. In 1460 the then Duke of York had his head 'spiked' here so that, as Queen Margaret says in Shakespeare's Henry VI: " . . . York may overlook the town of York."

This grim practice continued until the 18th century when the heads of Jacobites captured after the Rising of '45 were put on display. Seven years later two heads were still stuck up there but were stolen. The thief was caught and fined £5 and sent to jail for two years.

There were grim scenes outside these walls in 1644 when fleeing Royalists, survivors of the Battle of Marston Moor, clamoured in vain for entrance with the victorious Roundheads on their heels. In stark contrast Queen Elizabeth II was welcomed here in 1971 when the city celebrated its 1900th birthday. A museum within the bar sets out some of this history. (See page 43)

(At this point hardy souls can continue along the ramparts and complete a circuit of the Bar walls as set out in Walk Four.)

To continue Walk Three . . .

Leave the walls and enter Micklegate and head back towards the city. In times past this was the main road into York because it led directly to the city's only bridge. It was a trade route and over the centuries the rich merchants and businessmen built their homes along the

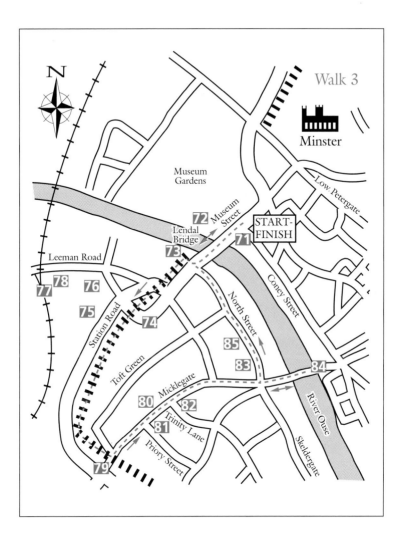

thoroughfare. It was also close to the dock area of the river. Medieval and Georgian entrepreneurs, however, would not have approved of the street's latest claim to fame, the Micklegate Run, a 'pub crawl' which takes drinkers from Micklegate Bar down to the river calling in at the other 'bars' on the way.

Notice **Micklegate House** (80) on the left regarded as one of the best of the Georgian town houses and thought to have been built by John Carr.

On the right outside **Holy Trinity Church** (81) is an unsolved mystery – a set of punishment stocks with only five foot holes – prompting one theory that it was reserved for two able-bodied and one one-legged beggar.

Down the hill on the right is **St Michael-cum-Gregory Church** (82) which dates back to 1170 but has Roman masonry in its tower. The medieval butter market used to be held here. On the left is another piece of railway history embodied in a street name. In Victorian times this was Hudson Street, named after the Railway King who was three times Lord Mayor of York. When he was disgraced for shady financial dealings it was renamed Railway Street and George's portrait was turned to face the wall in the Mansion House such was the city's sense of shame. But in 1971, on its 1900th birthday, York decided to forgive him. Railway Street disappeared and George Hudson Street returned.

Yet another church on the left, **St John**, Micklegate (83), built in the 14th and 15th centuries, has long since ceased to be a church but has been used as offices and as an arts centre.

Pause now amidst the traffic on **Ouse Bridge** (84) because this river crossing has been at the hub of the city's activities for centuries. The present bridge was built in the early part of the 19th century (taking more than ten years in the making) but there have been at least three on this site. The first was not just a bridge. Over the carriageway it had a prison, a toll booth, a chapel and public toilets – running water being readily available below. The weight was such that it must have been an accident waiting to happen and in 1154 it did.

Hundreds of people had gathered on the bridge to welcome Archbishop William into the city. The bridge collapsed but, according to ancient records, it was a 'miraculous disaster' because no-one was hurt. A second bridge, this time built of stone, also had housing on top including a council chamber. It was damaged by floods but was kept in being while the present bridge was under construction. Local builders wanted to get the stone by dismantling the city walls but Parliament refused permission.

Looking downstream on either side of the river is the city's former dockyard area – King's Staith on the left and Queen's Staith on the right. A few barges still ply their trade here but the area is mostly used by holiday craft.

Do not cross the bridge but take the elevated riverside walkway upstream. Alternatively go back a few yards and turn right into North Street and walk towards the Viking Hotel. On the left with its 120ft spire, fine stained glass and carved and painted ceiling is **All Saints**, North Street (85). The church is mainly 15th century in architecture but it is documented back to the 12th century. One of the windows dramatically tells the story of the world's end with fire and earthquakes. Try and find a man wearing medieval spectacles up among the angels in the south choir aisle glass. The carvings in the roof were restored in bright medieval-style colours some 20 years ago and were not to the taste of some critics. An anchorite's cell built in mock Tudor style was attached to the church at the turn of the century. Until twenty years ago a monk lived there in what was probably the smallest house in Britain. His presence followed a 15th century precedent when the church had a resident anchoress, a wise woman who was said to have been consulted by the Earl of Warwick, the Kingmaker.

From this point one can return to Lendal Bridge, the starting point for this walk, by walking along the river taking in a view across the water of the Guildhall.

And right around the Bar walls...

Start/finish: Lendal Bridge/Micklegate Bar with alternative finishing points.
See Walk Three to cover the first section from Lendal Bridge to Micklegate Bar.

Micklegate Bar

Continue along the ramparts from Micklegate Bar. This section of wall ends at **Baile Hill** (86) – a man-made mound thrown up by William the Conqueror and originally topped by a wooden tower – a twin for Clifford's Tower across the river. A later medieval stone tower on the hill disappeared in 1880 when local builders took the stone for bridge foundations.

Descending from the wall you can detour left into Skeldergate and visit the **Jorvik Brass Rubbing Centre** (87) (see page 43) before returning and crossing the river by Skeldergate Bridge. The **St George's** car park (88), downstream on the far bank, was the place for public spectacles at York's "popular price" – free. Public executions were so popular in the early 19th century that there were complaints that the railways were not putting on enough excursions to bring in the visitors.

Walk straight ahead and around the busy traffic roundabout and across Castle Mills Bridge. This bridge is over the River Foss and if you look to the right you will see the modern flood defence barriers which control the river before it joins the Ouse. To the left is the rear of the Law Courts and the Castle Museum. An old **water mill** (89) which was moved stone by stone from Raindale, North Yorkshire was re-erected here on the banks of the river as a working exhibit for the Museum.

Before returning to the ramparts at **Fishergate Postern** (90) you can detour into **St George's Churchyard** (91) where the highwayman Dick Turpin was finally laid to rest – at the second attempt. Body snatchers removed his corpse but it was retrieved, reburied and finally left in peace. Walk up the road to the left of the postern. The entrance to the church yard, which looks like a field, is round the corner on the left. The one, lonely gravestone is modern – the old one having been worn away.

At Fishergate Postern return to the parapet walk and pass the modern **Barbican Entertainment Centre** (92). At one time cattle were driven into the city at this point and sold from pens set up just outside the walls. The walk continues to **Walmgate Bar** (93) which is

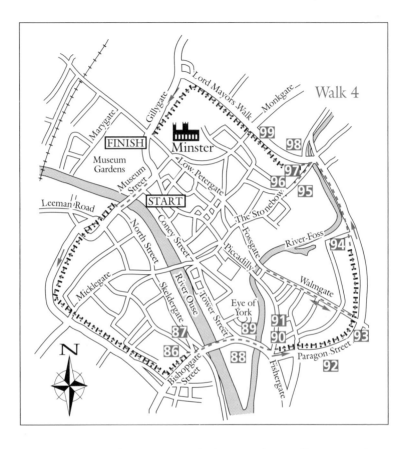

Walk 4

still complete with its protective barbican and portcullis. During the Civil War the Roundheads battered this gateway unmercifully with cannon and the shot marks can still be seen.

(If weary one can return to the city centre at this point by leaving the wall and walking back through Walmgate. More evidence of the Viking occupation of the city has recently been discovered in this area. In the 19th century large numbers of immigrant Irish families lived in poor conditions along Walmgate. At the turn of the century some 20 public houses were crammed into one short stretch of road.

Much has changed since then with shops, offices and homes moving back into the street.)

For those determined to walk round the city, continue along the wall until the ramparts come to an end at the brick built **Red Tower** (94). It was not thought necessary to continue the wall further at this point because of the marshy nature of the ground. The Normans had dammed the Foss to divert water into their fortress ditches and to create a Royal fishpond. Military access into the city here was therefore thought to be impossible. Leave the wall and walk along the busy internal ring road beside the river to the Foss Islands road junction.

A brief diversion … Turn left toward the city centre for about 100 yards to see and possibly call in at the black and white, timber-framed **Black Swan Public House** (95) – once a famous coaching inn and cock-fighting den. Cross over the road and on the opposite side is **St Anthony's Hall** (96) a former 15th century guildhall now used by York University for the storage and research of diocesan records.

A return can be made to the city centre at this point, otherwise … Walk back the way you have come on the hall side of the road passing **St Cuthbert's Church** (97) on the left. Although 16th century in origin

The Black Swan

it has been turned into an award-winning church administration centre by building a modern glass walled structure inside the old fabric.

At the restart of the ramparts on the corner of the busy Foss Islands crossroads rejoin the wall walk and head toward Monk Bar. The multi-storey car park that one sees outside the walls bears a plaque in English and Hebrew reminding visitors that on this site was once a Jewish cemetery. **Jewbury** (98) was the name given to the area after the Jewish community in the city acquired land here in the 12th century.

Looking inwards there is also a good view of the modern town houses which brought residential life back to the city centre at Aldwark. Nearing **Monk Bar** look over the parapet at a curious brick built "igloo" (99) set into the side of the ramparts. There is a "refrigerator servicing depot" of the 1800s – a place where ice was stored in a deep pit and sold to householders to keep their larders cool.

You are at Monk Bar. See Walk Two for the remaining stretch of wall up to Bootham Bar. If you have already covered this section you can return to the city centre from this point.

INFORMATION

Walk One

Minster – Open 7am to 8.30pm in summer and 7am to 5pm in winter. There is no entrance charge but a prominent display of collection boxes. Charges are made to visit the Chapter House, to climb the Central Tower and to visit the Foundations Museum and Treasury where Minster silver is on display and the remains of earlier cathedrals intermixed with the cathedral's modern concrete 'feet'. Entry to the cathedral is made by the North West Door and it is best to take a clockwise route leaving eventually by the South transept. Some highlights to look out for:

The West Window known as the Heart of Yorkshire because of the heart shape in the stone tracery

The Five Sisters Window in the North Transept – the oldest complete window in the Minster

The Astronomical Clock in memory of the thousands of airmen who died while flying from airfields in the North during World War Two

The Central Tower and crossing with its delicate Choir Screen

The world's largest area of stained glass – the Great East Window

The South Transept, destroyed by fire in 1984 and restored with a new carved and decorated ceiling which can be viewed without neck strain through mirrored tables

The 'basement' area showing the layers of history on the site

The Central Tower Roof reached after climbing 279 spiralling stone steps

Booklets and leaflets available either at St William's College or the Minster bookshop. (Map no 1)

ARC or Archaeological Resource Centre – Monday to Friday 10am-4.30pm. Weekends 1pm-4.30pm. A medieval church cleverly adapted to give visitors, particularly youngsters, a 'hands on' experience of archaeology. Trays of 'dig debris' are there to be sorted with knowledgable assistants on hand to help and explain. (Map no 15)

Merchant Adventurers' Hall – Open daily 8.30am-5pm. Closed Sundays November to late March. Much of the pageantry if not the power of the old guilds lives on in the dramatic timber framed building. It is still used for meetings of present day robe-clad guild members. (Map no 16)

41

Jorvik Viking Centre – Open April to October 9am-7pm. November to March 9am-5.30pm. On the exact spot where the walls of Viking York were found in the 1970s this hugely successful attraction was created in 1984. Time Cars take visitors back to the sights and smells of Viking times all reconstructed with impressive realism. (Map no 24)

Castle Museum – Weekdays 9.30am-5.30pm. Sundays 10am-5.30pm. Dr John Kirk saw a rural way of life disappearing when he worked as a doctor in Pickering. He made a collection of the everyday things that he saw and presented them to York in 1938 and the city displayed them in the former female and debtors' prison. Apart from the curiosities the buildings are fascinating in themselves with their tiny cells, massive locks and exercise yards now converted into Victorian and Edwardian streets. (Map no 27)

Regimental Museum (4th and 7th Dragoon Guards and the Prince of Wales' Own Regiment of Yorkshire) – Open Monday to Saturday 9.30am-4.30pm. Displays of uniforms and models of battles fought by the two regiments. (Map no 28)

Fairfax House – Open 1 March to 31 December 11am-5pm. Sunday 1.30pm-5pm. Closed on Fridays. Rescued from severe distress by the York Civic Trust this is now regarded as one of the finest Georgian Houses in the country. (Map no 29)

Mansion House – Although this is the home of the city's Lord Mayor while he is in office arrangements can be made to visit by writing to the Civic Secretary at the house. Apart from the staterooms there is a fine collection of civic silver and regalia including a Cap of Maintenance which the wearer is entitled to keep on his head in the presence of Royalty. (Map no 34)

Barley Hall – Open 1 March to 31 Oct, Monday to Saturday 10am to 4pm. Alderman William Snawsell, a goldsmith, lived here in the 15th century, and the building has been restored and fitted out with contemporary style furniture. (Map no 43)

Walk Two

St William's College – Open for viewing depending on which rooms are in use for functions. (Map no 50)

Treasurer's House – National Trust property. Open March to October daily (except Fridays) 10.30am-5pm. NT members free. Free access to tea room. (Map no 51)

Richard III Museum – Open Mar-Oct 9am-5pm. Nov-Feb 9.30-4pm. (Map no 55)

Merchant Taylors' Hall – Viewed by appointment only on Tuesdays between Easter and Autumn. Since its heydays as a centre of guild affairs it is now much in use for a variety of social functions. (Map no 54)

City Art Gallery – Open Monday to Saturday 10am-5pm. Sundays 2.30pm-5pm. As well as special exhibitions the gallery has its own collection of Old Masters. Picture and information 'treasure hunts' for children. (Map no 60)

King's Manor – Courtyards open daily. Admission elsewhere free depending on availability as this is a working part of York University. (Map no 61)

Yorkshire Museum – Open 10am-5pm, Sundays 1pm-5pm. Roman, Anglo-Saxon and Viking life in York are on display in the galleries and the museum is the venue for touring exhibitions and special displays. (Map no 69)

National Railway Museum – Open Monday to Saturday 10am-6pm, Sundays 11am-6pm. Locomotives old and nearly new, carriages and Royal saloons in what is arguably the biggest and best railway museum in the world. Sited on a former railway depot so some exhibits can and do slip out occasionally for a run on the main line. (Map no 70)

Walk Three

York Model Railway (next door to York Railway Station) – Open March to October, 9.30am-5.30pm. November to February, 10.30am to 5pm. Miniature trains chugging through miniature countryside. (Map no 78)

Micklegate Bar Museum – Open from 9am to dusk. (Map no 79)

Walk Four

Jorvik Brass Rubbing Centre, Skeldergate – Open 10am-5pm daily. Free entry but a charge made for rubbings. (Map no 87)

Tourist Offices

Exhibition Square. Tel: 01904 621756.
20 George Hudson Street. Tel: 01904 554488
Railway Station. Tel: 01904 621756

Car Parking

For all-day visiting it is best to use Park and Ride:
Askham Bar, off the A64 on the southern approach to York;
Clifton Moor, off northern section of outer ring road;
Grimston Bar, off eastern section of city bypass.
Long stay: Union Terrace, Foss Bank Multi-storey, St George's Field,
Nunnery Lane, Marygate. All likely to be full in high season.
Short stay car parks available nearer city centre but can be
expensive.

Banks

Most can be found in the Parliament Street area.

INDEX